HOMICIDAL PSYCHO JUNGLE CAT

Steven Haniford

HOMICIDAL PSYCHO JUNGLE CAT

A Calvin and Hobbes Collection by Bill Watterson

SCHOLASTIC INC.
New York Toronto London Auckland Sydney

ISBN 0-590-22210-4

18 17   5/0

Printed in the U.S.A.   14

First Scholastic printing, November 1994

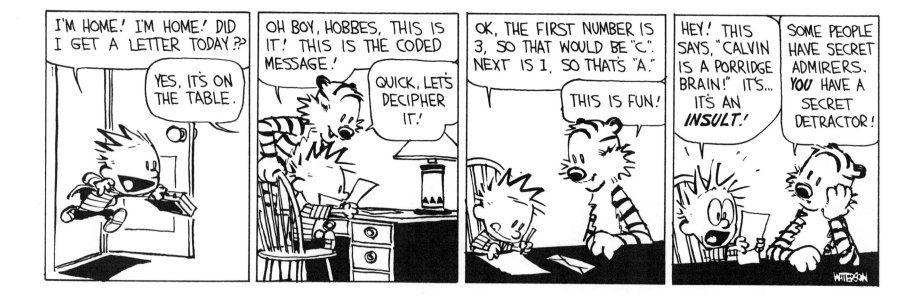

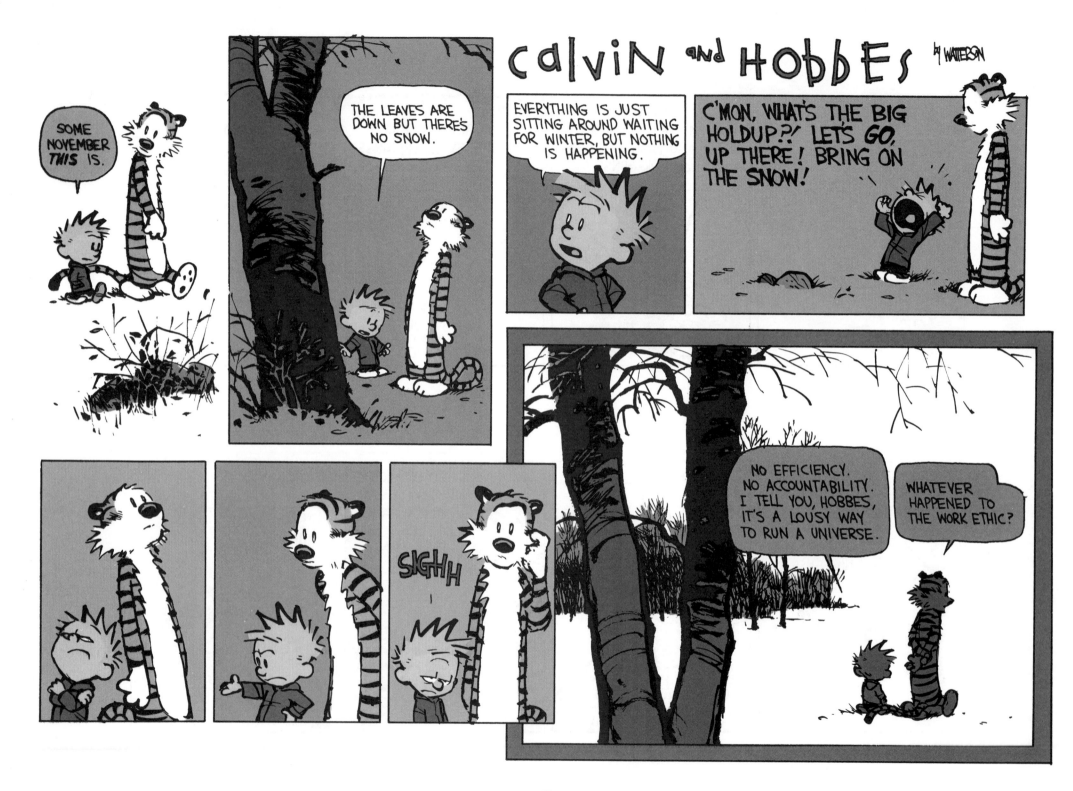

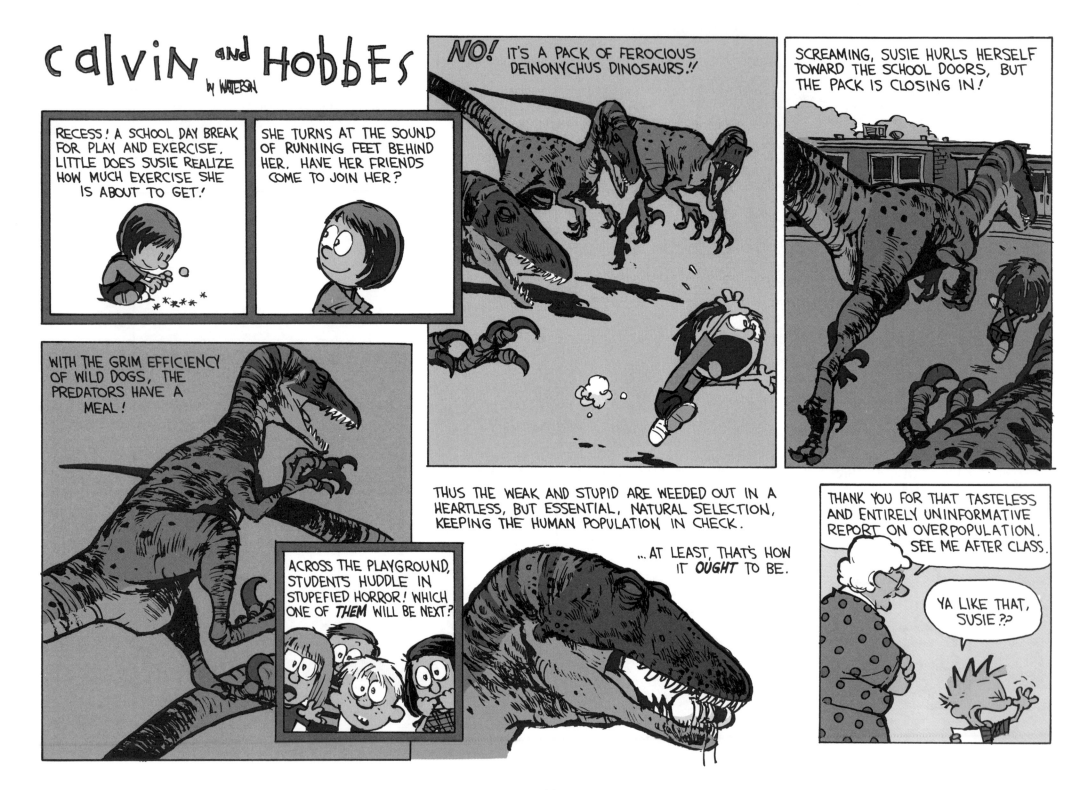

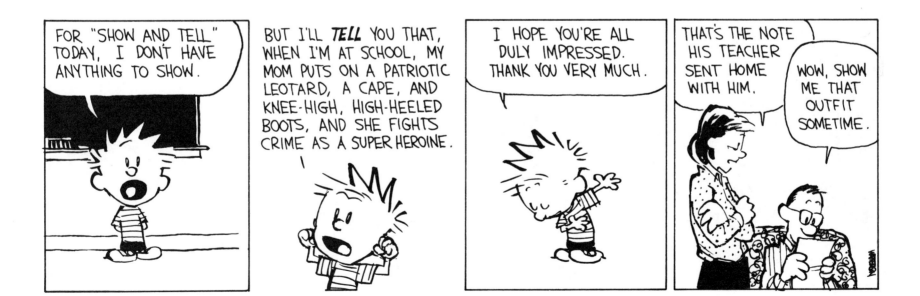

23

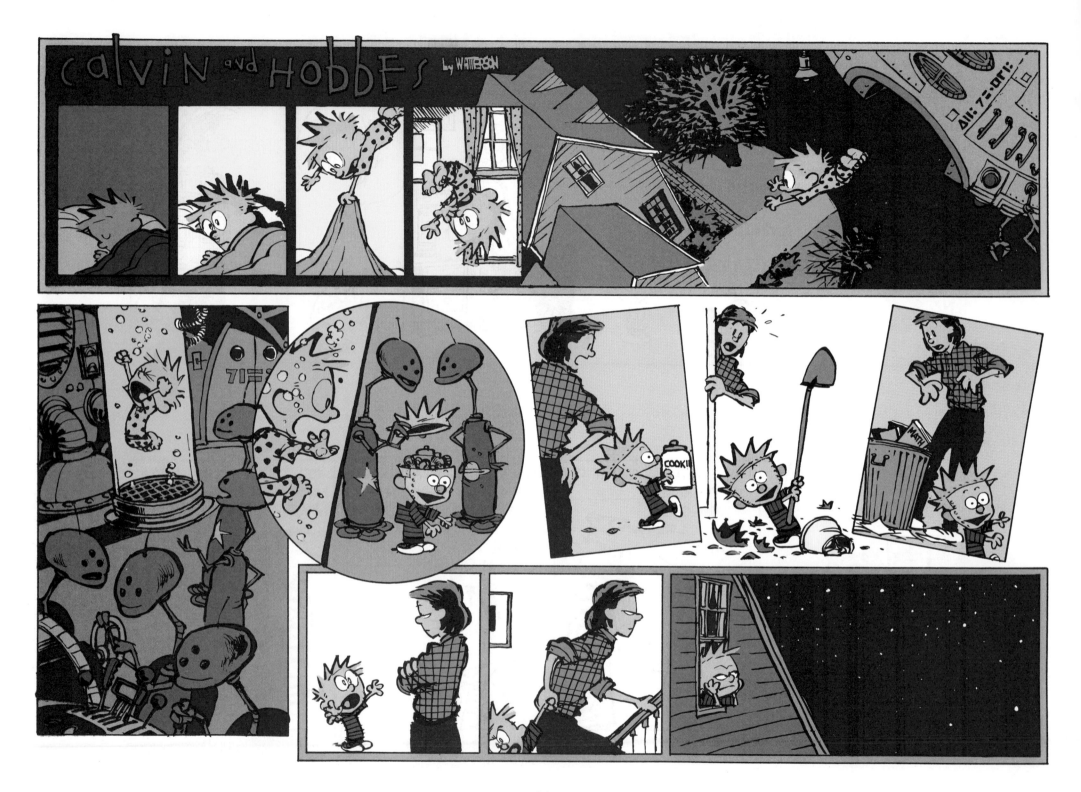

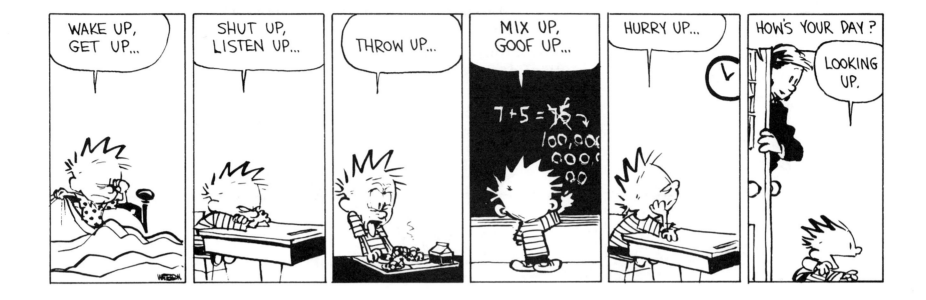

Dear Santa,
This year, I don't want any gifts. I just want love and peace for my fellow man.

39

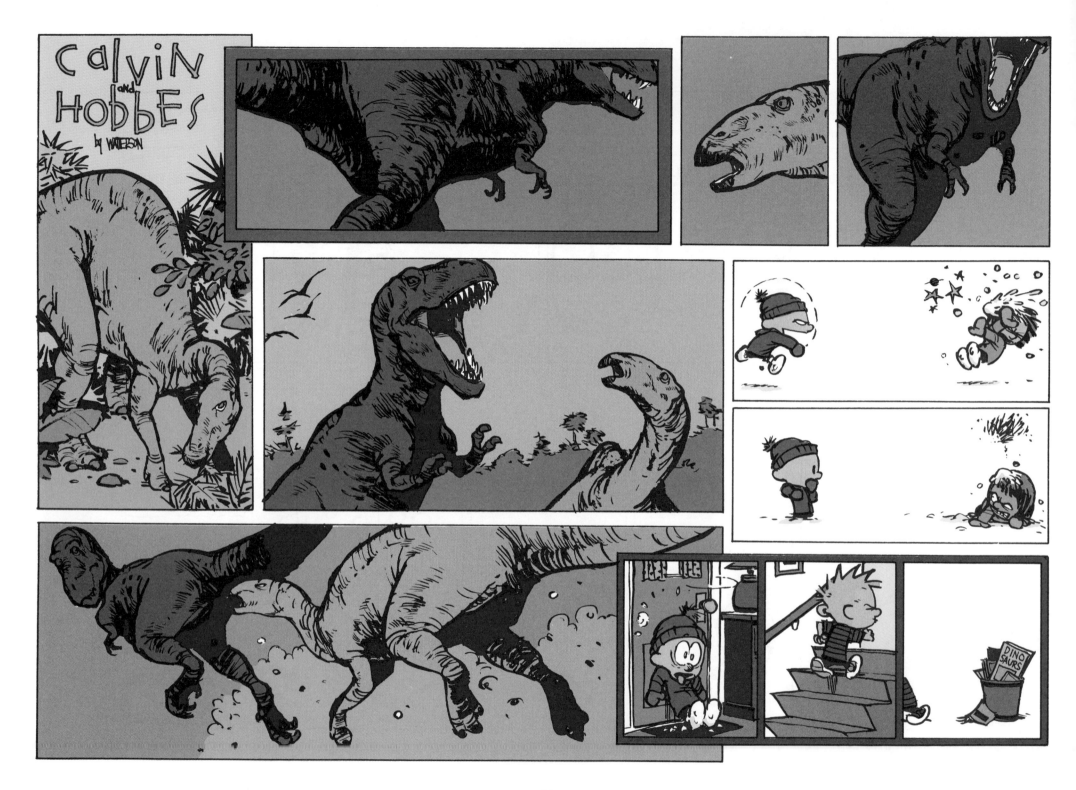

53

65

66

CALVIN and HOBBES by WATTERSON

..SIGHHHH..

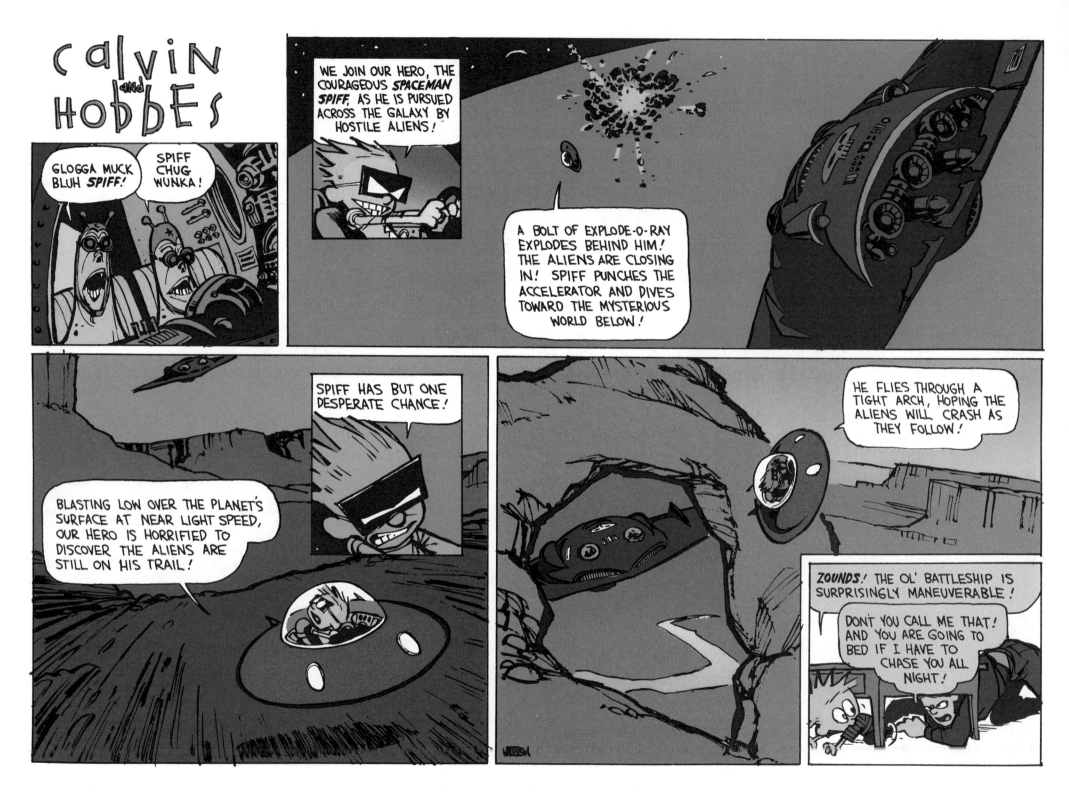

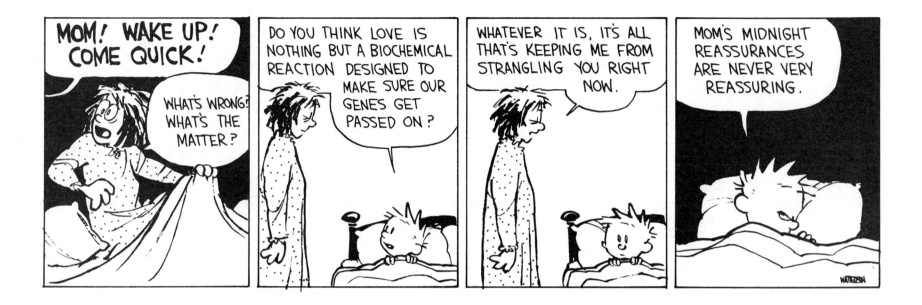

MISS WORMWOOD, I PROTEST THIS "C" GRADE! THAT'S SAYING I ONLY DID AN "AVERAGE" JOB!

I GOT 75% OF THE ANSWERS CORRECT, AND IN TODAY'S SOCIETY, DOING SOMETHING 75% RIGHT IS OUTSTANDING! IF GOVERNMENT AND INDUSTRY WERE 75% COMPETENT, WE'D BE ECSTATIC!

I WON'T STAND FOR THIS ARTIFICIAL STANDARD OF PERFORMANCE! I DEMAND AN "A" FOR THIS KIND OF WORK!

I THINK IT'S REALLY GROSS HOW SHE DRINKS MAALOX STRAIGHT FROM THE BOTTLE.

HISTORY WILL THANK ME FOR KEEPING THIS JOURNAL AT SUCH A YOUNG AGE.

AS ONE OF THOSE RARE INDIVIDUALS DESTINED FOR TRUE GREATNESS, THIS RECORD OF MY THOUGHTS AND CONVICTIONS WILL PROVIDE INVALUABLE INSIGHT INTO BUDDING GENIUS.

THINK OF IT! A PRICELESS HISTORICAL DOCUMENT IN THE MAKING! WOW!

..SO WHO *ELSE* SHOULD I ADD TO MY LIST OF TOTAL JERKS?

WHO ELSE DO YOU EVEN KNOW?

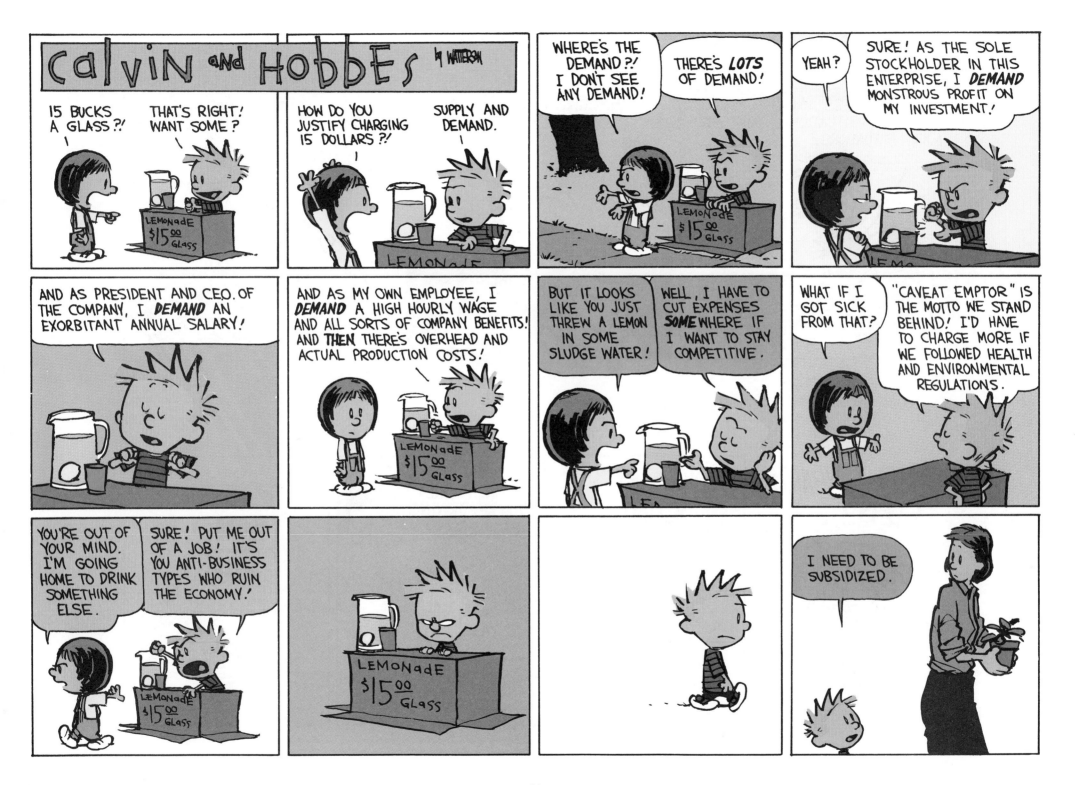

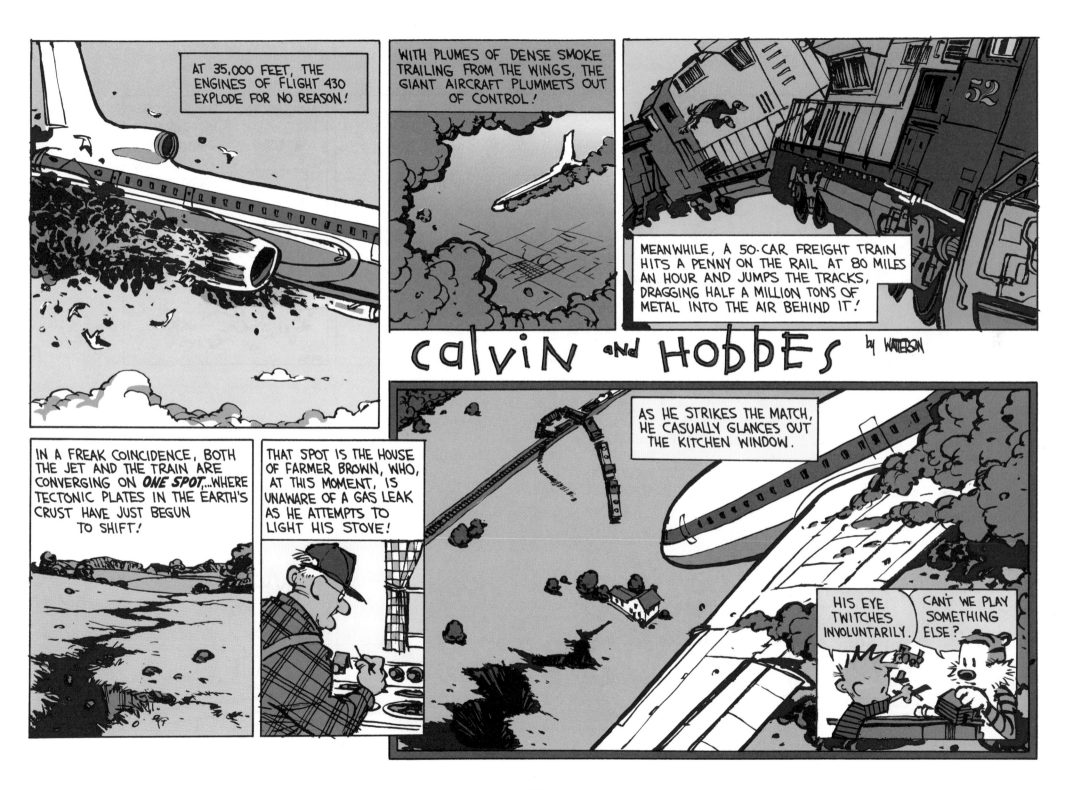

109

118

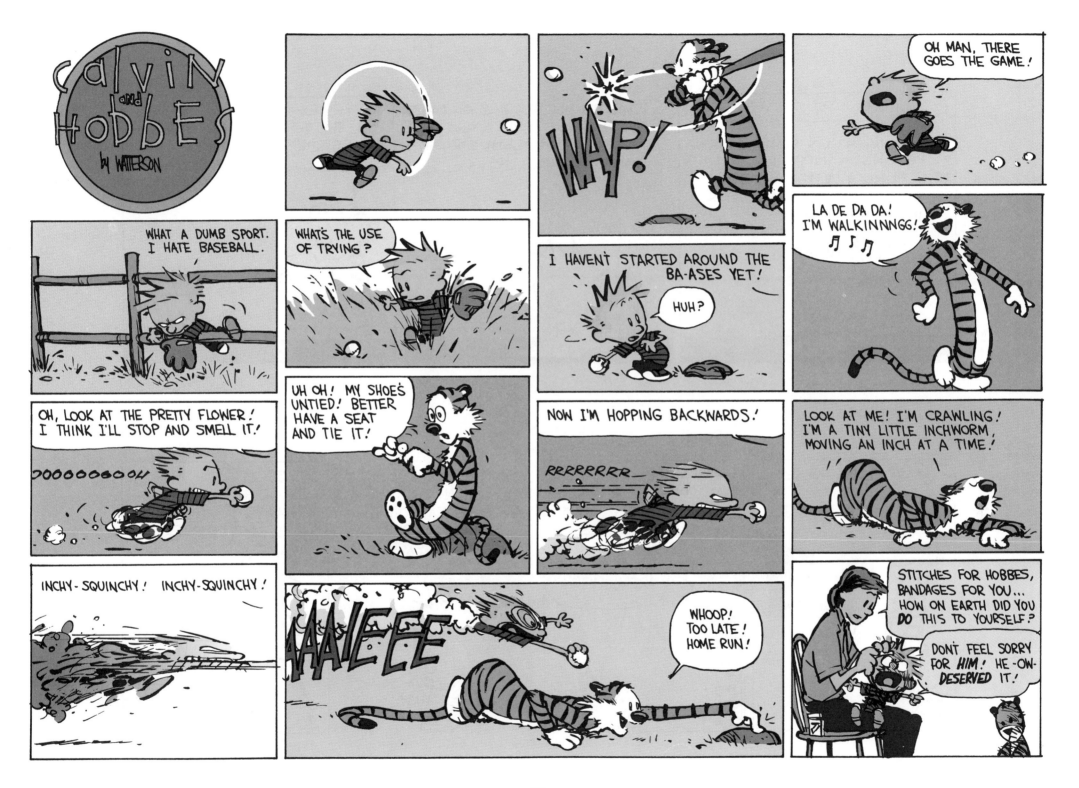

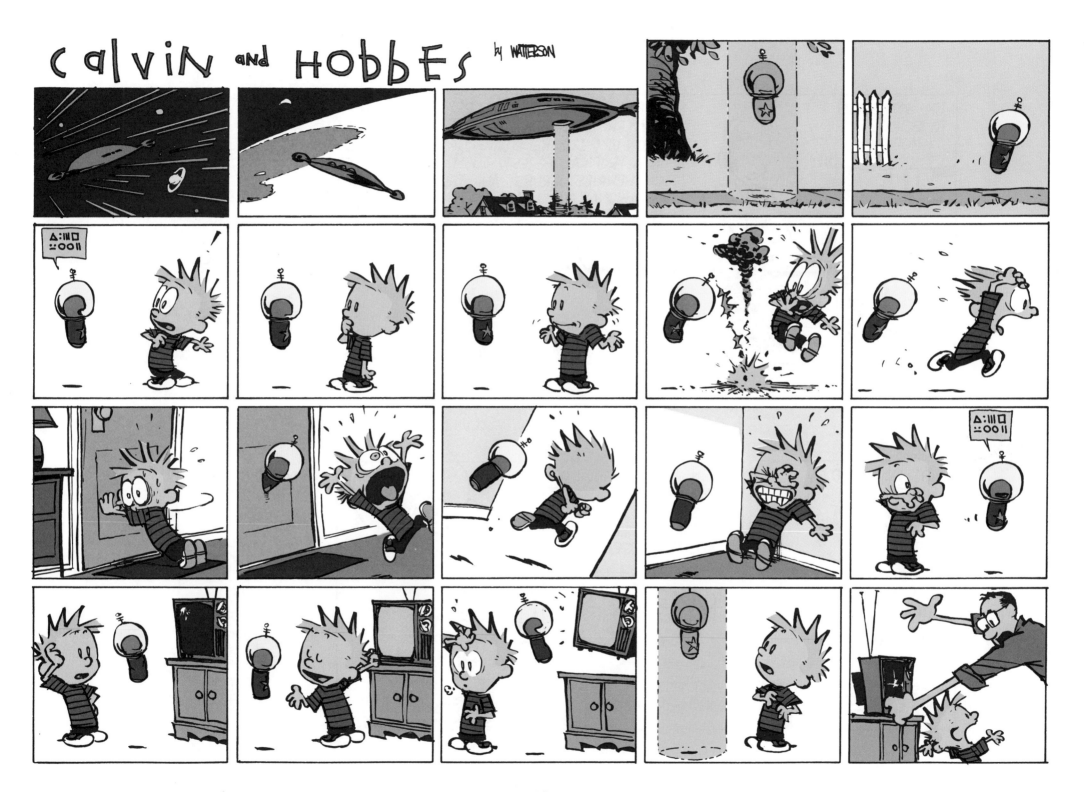

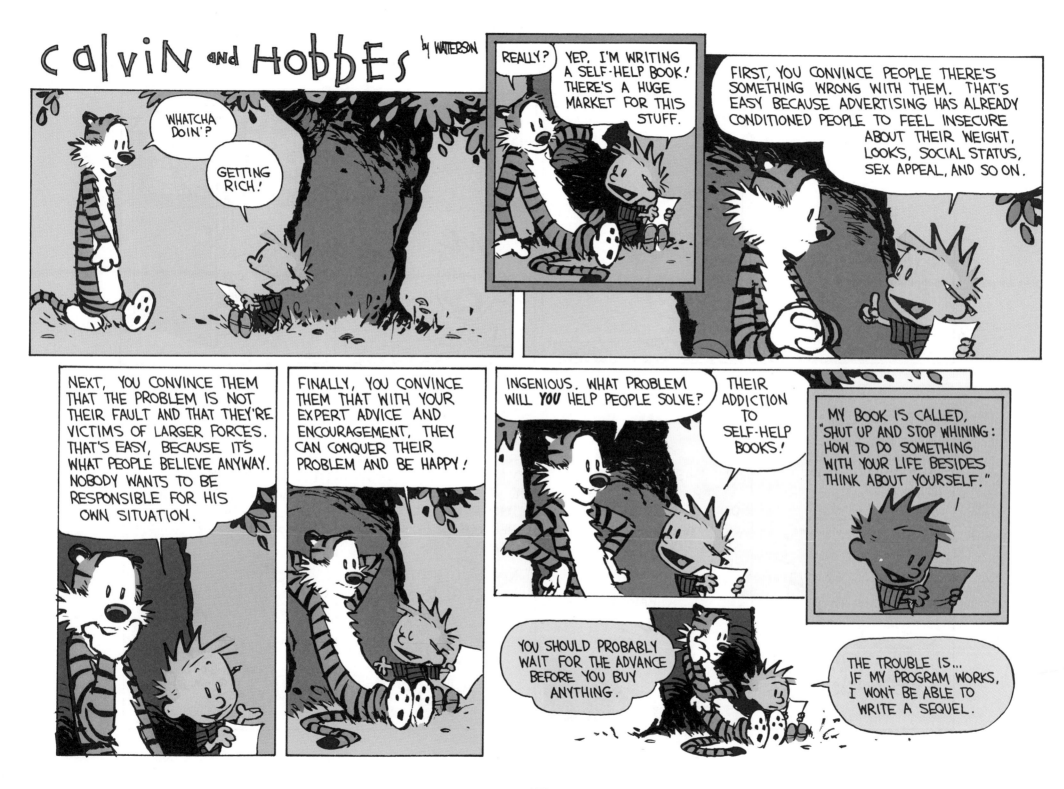

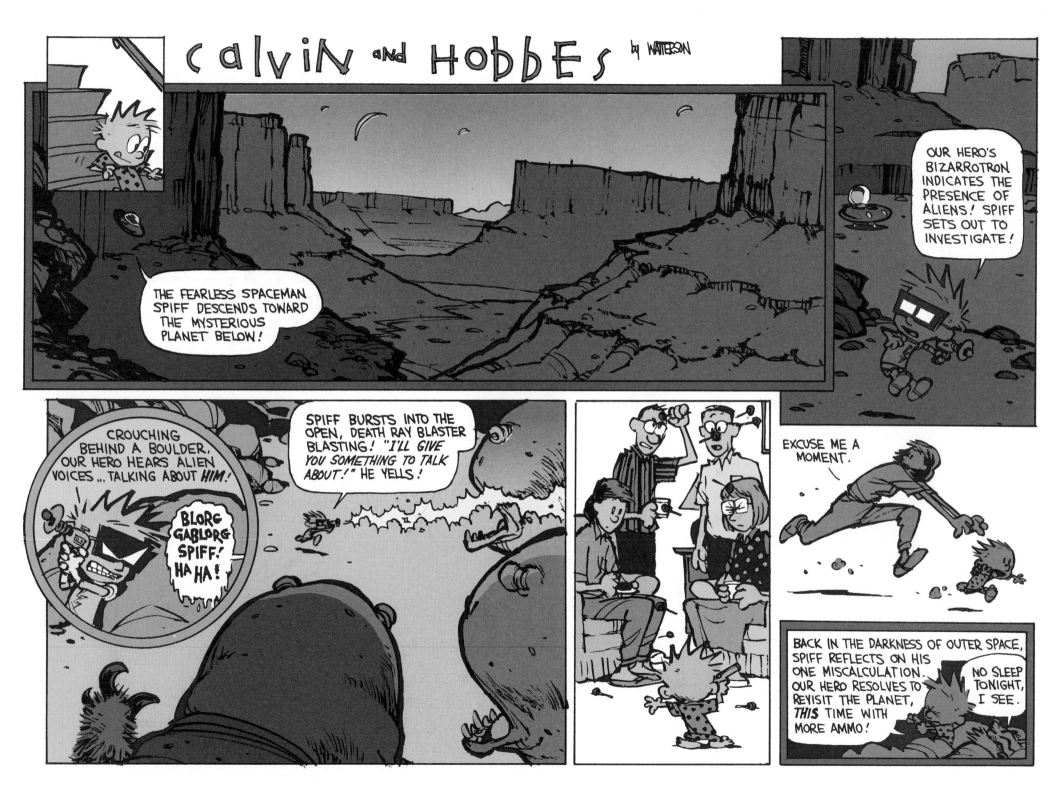

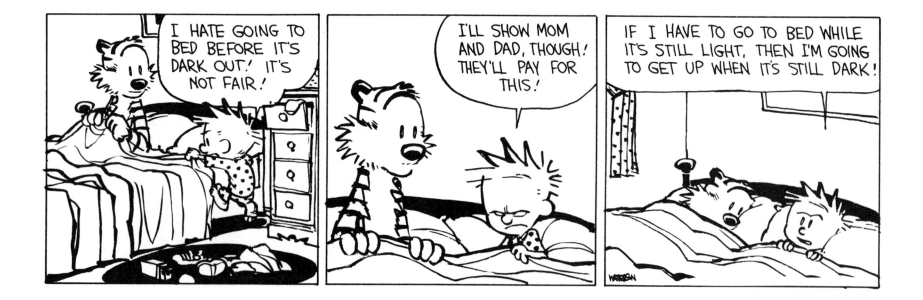

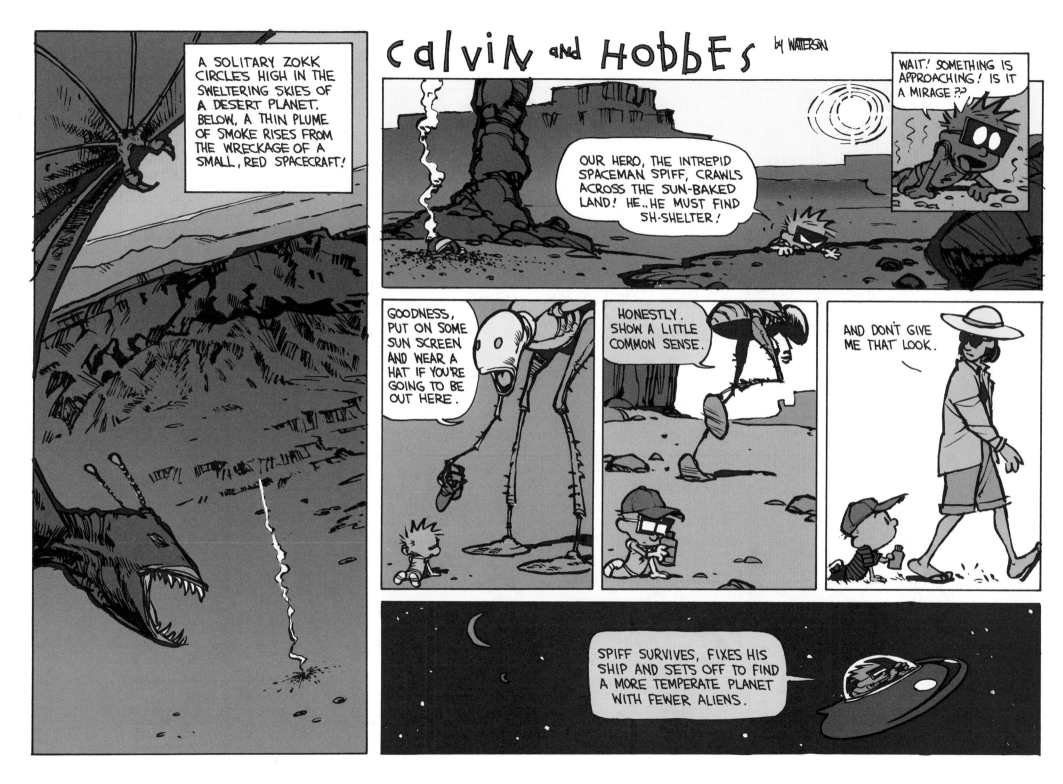

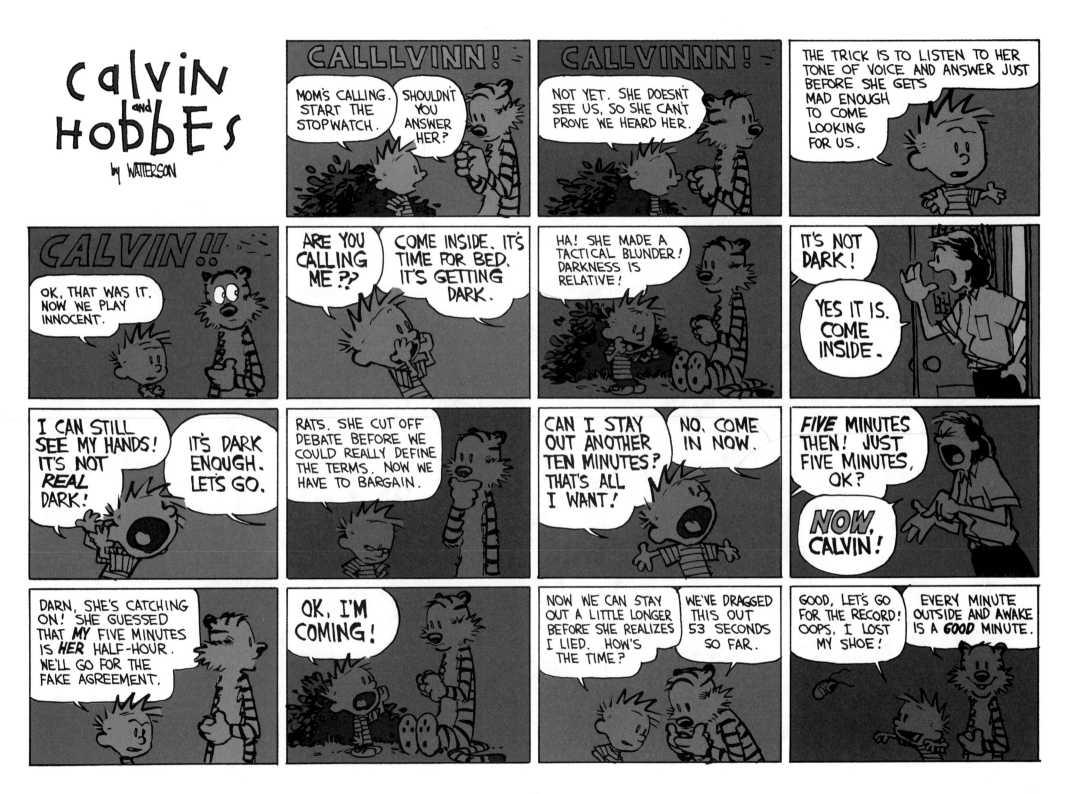

161

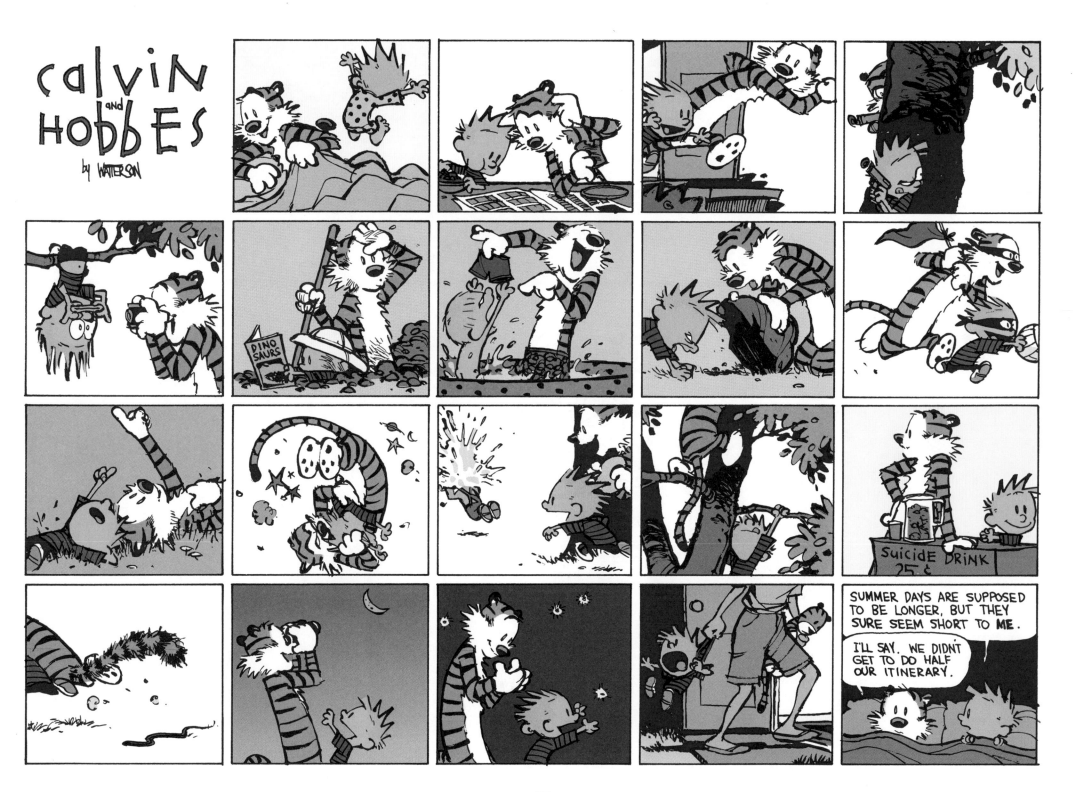